W9-BRS-660

THE COMPLETE

STAR WARS®

COOKBOOK

THE COMPLETE
STAR WARS®
COOK BOOK

TEXT BY ROBIN DAVIS
FRANKIE FRANKENY
WESLEY MARTIN

PHOTOGRAPHY BY FRANKIE FRANKENY

► WOOKIEE COOKIES, DARTH MALT, AND OTHER GALACTIC RECIPES

CHRONICLE BOOKS
SAN FRANCISCO

Originally published in two separate volumes as

Wookiee Cookies: A Star Wars Cookbook by Robin Davis,
photographs by Frankie Frankeny © 1998 by Lucasfilm Ltd. & ®

The Star Wars Cookbook II: Darth Malt and More Galactic Recipes
by Frankie Frankeny and Wesley Martin, photographs by Frankie Frankeny
© 2000 by Lucasfilm Ltd. & ®

This edition published exclusively for Barnes & Noble in 2010
by Chronicle Books LLC.

Art direction and concepts by Frankie Frankeny and Wesley Martin.
Food styling by Wesley Martin.
Props by Camella Haecker.
Series design by Daniel Carter.
Typeset in Bell Gothic, Clicker, and Univers.

ISBN: 978-1-4521-0103-3

Manufactured in Singapore.

10 9 8 7 6 5 4 3 2 1

Chronicle Books LLC
680 Second Street
San Francisco, CA 94107

www.chroniclebooks.com/custom
www.starwars.com

Table of Contents

Introduction

The Force inhabits all realms, including the kitchen. Its power is as present in the refrigerator as it is on the desolate ice planet Hoth. *The Complete Star Wars Cookbook* is full of culinary treats from the lush forests of Naboo, the sand-scourged outskirts of Tattooine, and the bustling city planet of Coruscant.

Some of the recipes here are simple enough to make on your own, while others require the help of a Master of the Force (otherwise known as Mom or Dad). In either case, it's always best to consult with an adult before trying something new. Adults, like Jedi Masters, know a great deal about the mysteries of the Force and will be able to guide you in your culinary pursuits.

Adventures await as you develop the skills you need to bring the life force of food to all who hunger for it. Accept the challenge, young Padawan, and remember that cooking should always be fun and always be safe. Let the wisdom of *The Complete Star Wars Cookbook* help you find your way and feel the Force!

BEFORE YOU BEGIN

It is important that you master some basic safety steps before you begin any project in the kitchen.

► An adult should always be present when you're cooking, especially if you are using knives, the stovetop, the oven, or tricky gadgets like food processors or blenders. Think of yourself as a Jedi apprentice, and of the adult as the Jedi Master. There's a lot of good stuff to learn from a Master.

► Shmi Skywalker would tell you to wash your hands well with soap and warm water before handling food or kitchen tools.

While you're cooking, stay alert. Reach out with your senses, and you'll find that you are able to prevent most kitchen mishaps. Here are some golden rules.

CONCENTRATE ON THE MOMENT

► Never run in the kitchen.
► Always wear shoes in the kitchen.
► Always keep everything—potholders, towels, packages of ingredients, this book, your fingers—away from burners on the stove. And remember, the stove may be hot even if the burners aren't on.

► Dry your hands thoroughly before turning on any electric switch or putting in or pulling out a plug.

► Wash knives and other sharp utensils one at a time. Don't drop them in a pan or bucket of soapy water—you may cut yourself when you reach into the water.

► Lift the lids of hot pots at an angle away from you, directing the rising steam away from your face.

► Use only dry potholders. Wet ones will conduct heat quickly and may burn you when you touch the handle of a hot pot.

► Put a pot or pan on the stove before you turn on the heat. Turn off the heat before you remove a pot or pan from the stove.

► Never put out a grease fire with water. Water causes grease to splatter and can spread the fire very quickly. To put out a grease fire, smother it with a tight-fitting lid or throw handfuls of baking soda on it.

ACT WISELY

► Never leave the kitchen while something is cooking.

► Keep pot handles away from the edge of the stove so the pots aren't easily toppled.

► Always position pot handles away from other stove burners. Otherwise, they'll get hot and burn you.

► Remove utensils from hot pots when you're not using them, placing them on a plate or spoon holder near the stove. Metal spoons and spatulas are especially dangerous because they'll absorb the heat and burn your hand when you go to use them.

► Start with a clean kitchen and keep it clean as you cook. If something spills, wipe it up right away. If you have time, wash dishes as you go.

► Turn off the blender's motor before removing the lid.

► Put ingredients away when you're finished with them.

► Know where to find the fire extinguisher and be sure it's in working order.

► Keep the fire department's number next to the phone.

The tools of the chef are powerful. Everything has a purpose. Treat all cooking equipment with the utmost respect and use items only for their intended purpose. Here's a list of what you might need:

TOOLS

Aluminum foil

Baking dishes

Baking sheets

Blender*

Cake pan

Can opener

Candy thermometer

Cheese grater

Colander

Cookie cutters

Cooling rack

Cutting board

Electric mixer*

Food processor*

Ice-cream scoop

Ice-cream maker

Ice-cube tray

Knives*

Ladle

Measuring cups and spoons

Mixing bowls of various sizes

Oven mitts

Paper cups

Parchment paper (for lining baking sheets)

Pastry brush

Plastic wrap

Pizza pan

Popsicle sticks

Potato masher

Potholders

Rolling pin

Saucepans with lids

Saute pan

Spatulas, rubber and metal

Stockpot

Strainer

Sifter

Skewers*

Skillet

Tea kettle

Toaster oven*

Tongs

Toothpicks

Vegetable peeler

Vegetable steamer

Waffle iron

Wax paper

Whisk

Wooden spoons

Zip-lock bags

*Use these items with extreme caution, and only with the help of a Master of the Force (Mom or Dad).

Go forth, young Jedi! May your Panakacakes be peanutty, may your Dark Side Salsa be spicy, and may the Force always be with you!

Breakfasts

Princess Leia Danish Dos

INGREDIENTS

	Butter for greasing baking sheet
	All-purpose flour for dusting work surface
1	tablespoon butter
1	10-oz package refrigerator pizza dough
2	tablespoons granulated sugar
$1\frac{1}{2}$	teaspoons ground cinnamon
1	tablespoon milk
$\frac{1}{3}$	cup confectioners' sugar, sifted
$\frac{1}{4}$	teaspoon vanilla extract

1. Preheat the oven to 350°F. Lightly grease a baking sheet.

2. Put the 1 tablespoon butter in a small saucepan. Set the pan on the stove and switch on the heat to low. When the butter has melted, turn off the heat.

3. Lightly flour a work surface. Unroll the pizza dough on top of the flour. Using a pastry brush, brush the melted butter over the surface of the dough.

4. Put the granulated sugar and cinnamon in a small bowl. Stir with a small spoon until well mixed. Sprinkle the cinnamon-sugar mixture over the dough, leaving a $\frac{1}{2}$-inch border on all sides.

5. Starting at a long side, roll up the dough into a log. Using your fingertips, pinch the seam together to seal.

6. Using a knife, cut the log crosswise into 1-inch-thick slices. Put the slices, cut side up, onto the greased baking sheet.

7. Using pot holders, put the baking sheet in the preheated oven. Bake until golden brown, about 20 minutes. Carefully transfer the baking sheet to the cooling rack. Cool 5 minutes. With a spatula, transfer rolls to the cooling rack and cool five minutes more.

8. Put the milk and confectioners' sugar in a small bowl. Stir with the spoon until a smooth frosting forms. Stir in the vanilla. Using a butter knife, spread frosting over the tops of the cinnamon rolls.
Makes about 10 rolls.

C-3PO Pancakes

INGREDIENTS

5	tablespoons unsalted butter
2	cans (8 $\frac{1}{4}$-ounces each) pineapple rings
1 $\frac{1}{4}$	cups all-purpose flour
2	tablespoons brown sugar
2	teaspoons baking powder
$\frac{1}{2}$	teaspoon salt
2	large eggs
1	cup milk
	Butter and maple syrup for serving

1. Preheat the oven to 250°F.

2. Put the butter in a small saucepan and switch on the heat to low. When the butter has melted, turn off the heat. Let the butter cool slightly (5 minutes).

3. Meanwhile, open the cans of pineapple. Drain off the juice from the cans into the sink. Set aside.

4. Put the flour, brown sugar, baking powder, and salt in a large bowl. Stir with a wooden spoon until well mixed.

5. Break the eggs into a medium bowl. Add the milk and 4 tablespoons of the melted butter. Whisk until well mixed. Slowly whisk in the flour mixture until well blended.

6. With a pastry brush, lightly brush some of the remaining melted butter in a large skillet. Set the skillet on the stove and switch on the heat to medium-high.

7. Fill a $\frac{1}{3}$-cup measuring cup with batter. When the skillet is hot, after 1 minute or so, pour in the batter. Cook the pancake until golden underneath and bubbles burst on the top, about 3 minutes.

8. Place 1 pineapple ring in the center of the pancakes. Using a spatula, carefully flip the pancake. Cook until golden brown on the second side, about 2 minutes longer. Transfer the pancake to a baking sheet. Using pot holders, put the sheet in the oven.

9. Repeat steps 7 and 8, brushing skillet with butter as needed. Serve the pancakes warm with butter and maple syrup.

Makes 8 pancakes.

Oola-la French Toast

INGREDIENTS

1	egg
¼	cup milk
1½	teaspoons sugar
⅛	teaspoon vanilla extract
¼	teaspoon cinnamon, or a pinch of ground cloves
3	bread slices
3	teaspoons butter
	Confectioners' sugar (optional)
	Butter and maple syrup for serving

1. Preheat the oven to 250°F.

2. Break the egg into a bowl. Add the milk, sugar, vanilla, and cinnamon or cloves. Beat with a whisk until blended. Pour into a shallow dish such as a pie pan.

3. Put bread slices into the egg mixture. Let sit for a few moments. With your fingers, turn the bread over and again let sit for a few moments. Both sides should look soaked with the egg mixture.

4. Put 1 teaspoon butter in a skillet. Put the skillet on the stove and switch on the heat to medium-high.

5. When the butter melts, pick up one piece of soaked bread and put it into the pan. Be careful not to burn your fingers. Fry until golden brown on the underside, about 3 minutes. To check, lift a corner with a spatula, and take a peek. If ready, use the spatula to turn it over. Now fry until golden brown on the second side, about 2 minutes longer.

6. With the spatula, move the toast to a baking sheet. Using pot holders, put the sheet in the oven.

7. Repeat steps 4, 5, and 6 to cook the remaining French toast.

8. Remove the sheet from the oven. (Don't forget to use the pot holders!) If desired, sprinkle the French toast with confectioners' sugar. Serve hot with butter and maple syrup.

Makes 1 or 2 servings.

Twin Sun Toast

Tattooine is a hot desert planet located in the outer reaches of the galaxy. It is home to young Luke Skywalker, who would sometimes gaze dreamily at the planet's twin suns.

INGREDIENTS

1	wide slice sourdough bread (at least 7 inches wide)
1	teaspoon butter
2	small eggs
	Salt and pepper to taste

1. Put the bread slice on a cutting board. Using a 2-inch round cookie cutter, cut out 2 holes, side by side, in the bread. Make sure to leave bread between and around holes.
2. Put a skillet on the stove and switch on the heat to medium. Put the butter in the skillet.
3. As the butter melts, spread it evenly on the bottom of the pan. Place the bread slice in the pan and break an egg into each hole. Sprinkle a little salt and pepper on the eggs. Fry until the clear part of the eggs turn white, 1 to 2 minutes.
4. Slip a spatula under the bread and flip it over quickly but carefully. Don't let the eggs slip out of the holes. Cook for 1 minute more. Slide the toast onto a plate. Serve at once.
Makes 1 serving.

Mos Eisley Morsels

INGREDIENTS

	Butter for greasing baking dish
2	cups all purpose flour
2	teaspoons baking powder
$1/2$	teaspoon baking soda
$1 1/2$	teaspoons ground cinnamon
1	teaspoon ground nutmeg
$1/2$	teaspoon ground cloves
$1/4$	teaspoon salt
3	large bananas
1	large egg
2	tablespoons vegetable oil
2	teaspoons vanilla

1. Preheat the oven to 375°F.
2. Lightly grease an 8-inch square baking dish.
3. Put the flour, baking powder, baking soda, cinnamon, nutmeg, cloves, and salt into a sifter. Sift the ingredients into large bowl.
4. In another large bowl, thoroughly mash the bananas with a fork or potato masher. Add the egg, vegetable oil, and vanilla, and stir until well blended.
5. Add the flour mixture and with a rubber spatula, mix the wet and dry ingredients together until just combined.
6. Pour the batter into the prepared baking dish and smooth the top of the batter with the spatula.
7. Using pot holders, place the baking dish in the oven and bake for 30-35 minutes, until a toothpick inserted into the center comes out clean. Using pot holders, transfer the dish to a cooling rack. Cut into squares.
Makes 12 morsels.

Variations: The morsels in the picture are topped with an extra mashed banana. If desired, mash a banana in a separate bowl, and spread on squares just before eating. Do not top the morsels with mashed banana unless you're going to eat them right away!

Sith Speeder Sunrise

If you want to know the secret behind Darth Maul's dexterity and determination, you just might find it in this nutritious breakfast. This wholesome speeder slice of juicy melon atop a dune of sweet, creamy oatmeal will keep you zipping around all day long.

INGREDIENTS

1½ cups milk

1   tablespoon honey

½   teaspoon cinnamon

¾   cup rolled oats

2   1-inch wedges cantaloupe

1. In a saucepan, bring the milk, honey, and cinnamon to a boil.
2. Add the oats and simmer for 6 to 8 minutes, stirring occasionally.
3. Transfer the oats to a bowl.
4. Cut a 1-inch-square piece of cantaloupe from one of the wedges and slice a V shape out of the melon without cutting through the rind.
5. Push the square "power pack" onto one end of the other melon wedge. You can secure it by driving a toothpick through the wedge and the power pack square.
6. Place the melon speeder on top of the "sand dune" of oatmeal and enjoy!
Serves 1

Boonta Classic Waffles

Start your engines with a winning plateful of these crisp golden waffles. Delicious served with Banana Butter.

WAFFLES

- 1½ cups all-purpose flour
- 1 tablespoon baking powder
- 1 tablespoon sugar
- 1 tablespoon brown sugar
- ½ teaspoon salt
- 3 large eggs
- 2 tablespoons melted butter
- 1½ cups milk
- 1 teaspoon vanilla

BANANA BUTTER

- 4 tablespoons butter, at room temperature
- 1 teaspoon sugar
- 1 ripe banana
- ½ cup crushed pistachios, walnuts, and pecans
- ¼ teaspoon cinnamon

1. Preheat waffle iron (a Belgian iron with large squares is best).
2. In a large bowl, whisk together the dry ingredients. Make a well in the center.
3. In a separate bowl, whisk together the eggs, butter, milk, and vanilla, then pour into the well of the dry ingredients.
4. With a wooden spoon, mix the batter until just combined. (A few lumps are okay.)
5. Pour ¼ to ½ cup batter into the hot iron and close the lid. Cook for 4 to 5 minutes, or until brown and crisp. Remove the waffle and repeat until batter is used up.
6. Spread the Banana Butter on the warm waffles.
7. Use crushed pistachios, walnuts, and pecans to make the spectators at the Podrace.

To make Banana Butter:
1. With a mixer, whip the butter, sugar and cinnamon together until soft.
2. In a separate bowl, mash the banana with a fork.
3. Add the banana to the butter mixture and whip until smooth.
Serves 6

Forceful Frittata

How feel you? Well, you'll feel *great* after a slice of this frittata. An elegant family breakfast, it's reminiscent of the decorative floor of the Jedi Council Chamber, where the great Jedi Masters convene to discuss the workings of the galaxy.

INGREDIENTS

6	eggs
1/2	cup milk
1/2	cup shredded mozzarella, 1 teaspoon reserved for topping
1/2	teaspoon salt
1/2	teaspoon pepper
1/2	cup of your favorite marinara sauce
15-20	fresh basil leaves

1. Preheat oven to 375°F.
2. Generously grease an 8-inch round cake pan.
3. In a large bowl, whisk together the eggs, milk, mozzarella (reserving 1 teaspoon), salt, and pepper.
4. Pour the egg mixture into cake pan and bake for 30 minutes on center oven rack. The edges of the frittata will just begin to brown.
5. Remove from oven and allow to cool for 2 to 3 minutes.
6. Place a flat plate or tray over the cake pan and flip the frittata onto the plate.
7. Spread the marinara sauce in the center of the frittata in a 3-inch circle. Sprinkle the reserved teaspoon of shredded mozzarella on the tomato sauce, and place the basil leaves around the edges to recreate the Jedi Chamber floor.
8. Cut into wedges and serve.
Serves 4 to 6

Booma Breakfast Tarts

Organic energy gives the Booma their mysterious power. You can energize yourself with these delicious breakfast tarts!

INGREDIENTS

1	egg
3	tablespoons sugar
1	frozen pie-crust shell, thawed
1/4	cup blueberry jam
1	tube lavender cake-decorating icing with a small tip (optional)

1. Preheat oven to 375°F.

2. Crack the egg into a small bowl and beat it with a fork until well mixed.

3. Sprinkle 1 tablespoon of the sugar on the work surface.

4. Turn the pie-crust shell over onto the sugared work surface. Carefully press the crust down, being careful not to tear it. Sprinkle another tablespoon of sugar on top of the crust. With a rolling pin, gently roll over the crust to press the sugar in—try not to roll the crust any thinner.

5. Using a large oval cookie cutter, cut out six ovals. Transfer three to a parchment-lined baking sheet. With a pastry brush, brush egg mixture around the edges of each oval, covering only about 1/4 inch of the edge with egg. Place 1 teaspoon of the jam on each oval and spread it out to where the egg wash begins.

6. With the smallest round cookie cutter you have, or a small knife, cut a small circle out of three of the ovals right in the center. Place these three ovals over the first three ovals. With your finger, gently press the edges of the tart together to seal them.

7. Brush the top of each tart with the remaining egg mixture. Sprinkle additional sugar on each tart.

8. Bake for 15 minutes, or until golden brown.

9. Decorate with the icing after tarts have cooled.

Makes 3 tarts

Handmaiden Hash Browns

These savory hash browned potatoes have an understated elegance, just like the handmaidens. Wedges of this crispy potato cake make a fantastic accompaniment to a slice of Forceful Fritatta.

INGREDIENTS

2	large russet potatoes
1	small red pepper, seeded and finely chopped
2	tablespoons vegetable oil
	Salt
	Pepper
	Grated cheddar cheese (optional)

1. Peel the potatoes and rinse in cold water.
2. Grate the potatoes using the large holes on a cheese grater, or a food processor fitted with a grater attachment. Keep your fingers away from the grater! Place the grated potatoes in a colander, rinse well with cold water, and drain. Toss with the chopped red pepper.
3. Heat 1 tablespoon of the oil in a large skillet over medium heat. Spread the grated potatoes in a thin, even layer in the skillet. Using a spatula, press the potatoes into the pan. Fry the potatoes for approximately 8 minutes, or until the bottom turns golden brown.
4. Remove the pan from the heat. Place a large plate or tray over the skillet and carefully flip the potato cake onto the plate. Pour the remaining tablespoon of oil onto the skillet. Carefully slide the potato cake into the pan so the unbrowned side faces down. Return skillet to the heat. Fry for another 8 minutes, or until the other side turns golden brown.
5. Season to taste with salt and pepper. Sprinkle with cheese, if desired. Cut into wedges and serve.
Serves 4

Snacks and Sides

Star Wars Pretzels
Pickle Jar Jar
Tongue-Numbing Nachos
Amidala Challah
Boss Nass Broccoli
Bubble City Salad
Tusken Raider Taters
Jabba Jiggle
Jedi Juice Pops
Dark Side Salsa
Ewok Eats
The Force Fruit Fun
Darth Maul Dip

Star Wars Pretzels

Crispy on the outside and soft on the inside, these salty and delectable pretzels take on added magic when they spell out those two winning words: *Star Wars*.

INGREDIENTS

1	package (11 ounces) refrigerator bread sticks (8 sticks of dough)
¼	cup water
2	tablespoons coarse salt crystals

1. Preheat oven to 375°F.
2. Open bread-stick package, unroll dough, and separate.
3. On a parchment-lined baking sheet, spell out S-T-A-R W-A-R-S with the dough. It should take one bread stick per letter. Cut the dough when necessary to make the letters.
4. Brush each letter with water and sprinkle coarse salt all over the letters.
5. Bake for 10 to 15 minutes, until golden brown.
6. Arrange the letters on a dark-colored plate or platter (if you have one) and serve with mustard. You can also sprinkle coarse salt on the plate to make the stars.

Pickle Jar Jar

Jar Jar shouldn't have any trouble getting his tongue around these sweet-and-sour refrigerator pickles, and neither should you.

INGREDIENTS

2	cups distilled white vinegar
1	cup sugar
2	large cucumbers
3	large carrots, peeled
2	cloves fresh garlic

1. In a large bowl, whisk together the vinegar and sugar until dissolved.
2. Wash the cucumbers and carrots. Cut each cucumber in half lengthwise, then each half into three spears. Cut the carrots in half lengthwise, then each half again lengthwise. Trim the carrots to fit the jar you use.
3. Pack the cucumbers and carrots together in quart-size jars. (Mayonnaise jars work great. You'll need two for this recipe.) Slice the garlic cloves into thin slices and add to each jar. Pour the liquid over the cucumbers and carrots until completely covered. If you run out of liquid, top off each jar with cool water.
4. Refrigerate for at least 2 days.
5. Remove cucumbers and carrots from jars with a fork or your fingers and enjoy!
Makes 2 quart jars

Tongue-Numbing Nachos

This wondrous pile of tortilla chips, beans, lettuce, cheese, and olives will satisfy any appetite, extraterrestrial or otherwise. But be cautious with the jalapeños. Too many of those can be as dangerous as Podracing!

INGREDIENTS

½	bag (14 ounces) tortilla chips
1	can (15 ounces) refried beans
½	cup of your favorite salsa
1	cup shredded jack or cheddar cheese, or a combination of both
1	small can sliced black olives, drained
1	tablespoon jarred jalapeños, diced
1	cup shredded lettuce

1. Preheat oven to 350°F.
2. On a large cookie sheet, arrange the chips in one even layer.
3. In a bowl, stir the refried beans with 1 tablespoon of the salsa to thin them. With a spoon, drop the beans onto the chips as evenly as possible.
4. Sprinkle the cheese evenly over the beans. Then sprinkle the olives and diced jalapeños over the top of the cheese.
5. Bake for 12 to 15 minutes, or until cheese is melted and bubbly.
6. Remove from oven. Sprinkle the lettuce and remaining salsa over the top.
7. Serve using a spatula.
Serves 4 to 6

Amidala Challah

This recipe is no cakewalk—it will take about 5 hours total. But if you have some time on your hands and a little patience, you can make two beautiful loaves of braided, buttery bread fit for a queen. Be sure to ask your Jedi Master for help!

INGREDIENTS

2	tablespoons yeast
2 1/4	cups lukewarm water
2/3	cup maple syrup
3	beaten eggs
1/2	cup butter
1	tablespoon salt
7-8	cups unbleached all-purpose flour
1	beaten egg for wash
1	tablespoon poppy seeds and/or sesame seeds
1	teaspoon coarse salt

1. Dissolve the yeast in the water. Add the maple syrup, eggs (reserving 2 tablespoons), butter, and salt and mix well.
2. Gradually add the flour.
3. Knead the dough on a floured board until elastic, about 8 minutes. Place in a greased bowl and cover with a cloth. Let the dough rise until doubled, about 1 hour.
4. Divide the dough into six parts. Roll three parts into long strips and braid together, sealing the ends to make one loaf. Repeat with the remaining three parts.
5. Cover the loaves with cloth and allow to rise until doubled.
6. Preheat oven to 350°F.
7. Brush with beaten egg wash and sprinkle with seeds and salt.
8. Bake on a greased sheet for 45 to 50 minutes, until golden brown. With oven mitts, carefully lift one loaf and tap the bottom with your knuckle. It will make a hollow thudding sound if it's done.
Makes 2 loaves

Boss Nass Broccoli

Here's a secret: when Boss Nass was a little Gungan, he didn't much care for green veggies like broccoli. But broccoli in the shape of himself plus a zesty, cheesy sauce definitely changed his mind. And now he's the most important Gungan of all!

INGREDIENTS

1	head fresh broccoli
$1/4$	cup shredded parmesan
1	cup cubed American cheese
$1/2$	cup milk
$1/2$	cup smoky barbecue sauce in a squeeze bottle

1. Using a vegetable steamer insert, steam the whole broccoli head in a stockpot until tender, 6 to 8 minutes.

2. To make Boss Nass's crown, sprinkle the parmesan into an 8-inch nonstick sauté pan. Form the parmesan into a triangle in the pan, making sure the cheese is spread evenly. Place the pan over medium heat and allow the parmesan to cook and melt. When the cheese is bubbly and starts to brown on the underside, remove pan from heat. Slide the parmesan crisp onto a work surface. Carefully mold the triangle into a cone shape by rolling one side of the triangle to meet another side. Don't burn yourself! Press the seam with your fingers and hold in place until the parmesan crisp hardens and holds its shape.

3. In a saucepan or a bowl in the microwave, heat and stir the cubed American cheese and milk together until the cheese is melted and the sauce is smooth.

4. Place the steamed broccoli on a plate. Spoon the cheese sauce around the broccoli and place the parmesan crown on top of it. Squeeze swirls of the barbecue sauce onto the cheese sauce to look like Boss Nass' coat and draw the indentations in his crown.

Serves 2

Bubble City Salad

This shimmering salad evokes Otoh Gunga, the magnificent underwater city. Use a knife to serve up some Gungan-size slices of this cool, refreshing salad.

INGREDIENTS

1	large package lemon or pineapple Jell-O
3	cups water
2	packages unflavored powdered gelatin
1	can lemon-lime soda
12	large green grapes, washed
	Orange slices (optional)

1. In a mixing bowl, mix together the Jell-O and gelatin. Bring 2 cups of the water to a boil. Pour the boiling water over the Jell-O mixture and stir until dissolved. Add the remaining cup of cold water and the can of soda and stir.

2. Pour the Jell-O into the tallest, narrowest bowl you have and place it in the refrigerator.

3. After the Jell-O has set for about $1\frac{1}{2}$ hours, remove from the refrigerator. Using the handle of a wooden spoon, press the grapes into the Jell-O, suspending them at even intervals.

4. Put the Jell-O back into the refrigerator and allow to set completely.

5. When ready to unmold, dip the tall, narrow bowl into a sink or larger bowl full of hot water for 10 seconds. The Jell-O should release itself from the mold. Place a plate on top of the Jell-O mold and carefully flip it over.

6. Serve Bubble City with orange slices, if desired.

Serves 4 to 6

Tusken Raider Taters

Tusken Raiders are fierce, mysterious creatures who wander the Tatooine desert, climbing sand dunes that look mysteriously like these potato dunes.

INGREDIENTS

1	teaspoon salt
1	pound purple or russet potatoes
$1/4$	cup milk
2	tablespoons butter
	Salt and pepper to taste

1. Fill a large saucepan two-thirds full with water. Add the salt.
2. Using the vegetable peeler, peel the potatoes. Put a peeled potato on the cutting board. Cut the potato in half lengthwise. Holding a potato half cut side down, slice it lengthwise into 1-inch slices. Now hold the slices and cut across them in the opposite direction to make 1-inch pieces. Be sure to keep your fingers clear of the knife blade. Add the potato to the pan. Repeat with the remaining potatoes.
3. Put the pan on the stove and switch on the heat to high. Bring the water to a boil and boil the potatoes, uncovered, until tender, about 10 minutes. (You can check by scooping out a potato cube with a slotted spoon, and poking the cube with a fork. It should go in easily.) Turn off the heat.
4. Put the colander in the sink. Remove the pan from the stove and pour the water and potatoes into the colander. Be very careful; the steam from the boiling water can burn you.
5. Return the potatoes to the pan. Mash with a potato masher. Add the milk and butter. Continue to mash until the butter and milk are mixed in. Potatoes can be as smooth or lumpy as you like. Season to taste with salt and pepper.
Makes 2 servings.

Variation: If you want brown potatoes like the ones in the picture, mash russet potatoes with 2 tablespoons of soy sauce.

Jabba Jiggle

This green, fruity treat wiggles and jiggles just like Jabba.

INGREDIENTS

1   can (11-ounces) mandarin orange segments

1   can (8-ounces) crushed pineapple in juice

1   package (6-ounces) lime Jell-O®

2   cups cold water

1   cup seedless grapes

1. Open the cans of mandarin oranges and crushed pineapple. Drain off the juice from the cans into the sink.
2. Fill a tea kettle with water. Put the kettle on the stove and switch on the heat to high. Bring the water to a boil and remove from the heat.
3. Open the Jell-O® package and empty it into a large mixing bowl. Carefully measure 2 cups boiling water and pour them over the Jell-O®. Stir with the wooden spoon until the Jell-O® dissolves completely. Then stir in the cold water.
4. Add the drained mandarin oranges, pineapple, and the grapes. Stir until well mixed.
5. Pour the mixture into a glass bowl. Refrigerate until firm, about 2 hours.
Makes 8 servings.

Jedi Juice Pops

INGREDIENTS

14   small fresh or frozen strawberries

1¼ cups fruit juice, such as orange, cranberry,
      apple, fruit punch, or lemonade

1. If you are using fresh strawberries, cut off their
stems with a small knife. Place 1 strawberry in
each ice-cube compartment of an ice-cube tray.
Fill the ice-cube tray with the juice.
2. Put the tray in the freezer and freeze until
almost firm, about 2 hours.
3. Push a popsicle stick (or a toothpick) into
the center of each cube, through the strawberry.
Return to the freezer and freeze until firm,
about 1 hour longer.
4. Pop out the juice bars and eat!
Makes 14 pops.

Variation: You can use banana slices, seedless
grapes, or orange segments cut into chunks
instead of strawberries.

Dark Side Salsa

INGREDIENTS

6	ripe Roma tomatoes
1	small onion
1	small avocado
1	can (4 ounces) diced mild green chiles
1	cup frozen corn, thawed
1	lemon or lime
	Salt and pepper to taste
	Blue corn tortilla chips

1. Put a tomato on the cutting board and cut out the green stem. Cut the tomato in half from the top to the bottom. Holding a tomato half cut side down, slice it lengthwise into thin slices. Now cut the slices into little cubes. Put the tomato cubes in the mixing bowl. Repeat with the remaining tomatoes.

2. Put the onion on the cutting board. Carefully slice off the root end and the stem end. Strip off the dry brown skin. Then cut the onion in half from the top to the bottom. Holding an onion half cut side down, thinly slice it crosswise. Now hold the slices together and cut across them in the opposite direction. Be sure to keep your fingers clear of the knife blade. Add the onion to the tomatoes.

3. Pit the avocado by carefully cutting it in half around the pit. Pull the halves apart and carefully scoop out the pit with a spoon. Peel the skin from the avocado with your fingers. Place the avocado half cut side down on the cutting board. Cut it lengthwise into thin slices, then cut the slices into little cubes. Repeat with the remaining avocado half. Add the avocado to the tomatoes and onions.

4. Open the can of chiles. Drain off the liquid from the can into the sink. Add the chiles to the mixing bowl. Then add the thawed corn.

5. Put the lemon or lime on the cutting board and cut it in half. Hold a half in your hand and squeeze it over a tablespoon until the tablespoon is full of juice. Add the juice to the mixing bowl.

6. Stir together everything in the bowl until well mixed. Add the salt and pepper to taste. Serve with the tortilla chips.

Makes 4 servings.

Ewok Eats

INGREDIENTS

6	fresh herb sprigs, a combination of parsley, thyme, and chives
1/2	cup plain yogurt
4	ounces cream cheese, at room temperature
1	teaspoon Worcestershire sauce
1/4	teaspoon garlic salt
1	teaspoon pepper
1	head broccoli

1. With your fingers, pull the thyme and parsley leaves off the stems. Put the leaves and chives on the cutting board and carefully chop with a knife. Set aside.
2. Put the yogurt and cream cheese in the mixing bowl. Stir with the wooden spoon until smooth. Add the chopped herbs, Worcestershire sauce, salt, and pepper and stir well. Cover with plastic wrap and refrigerate for 1 hour to give the flavors time to blend.
3. Put the head of broccoli on the cutting board. Use the knife to cut off the florets (the flowery looking tops). Be sure to leave a little stem on the florets. If the florets are in big clusters, cut between the stems to make smaller ones.
4. Spread the dip in the bottom of a shallow dish such as a pie pan. Stand the florets upright in the dip, side by side to make an Ewok forest.
Makes 4 servings.

Variation: You can also serve the dip with potato chips, tortilla chips, or other vegetables such as carrot and celery sticks.

The Force Fruit Fun

INGREDIENTS

2   cups strawberries, bananas, or blueberries,
     or a combination of the three

2   teaspoons lemon juice

3   tablespoons sugar

1. Preheat oven to 225°F.
2. Wash the fruit. Remove strawberry stems with a knife and peel
the bananas, if using.
3. Place fruit in a blender. Put the lid on the blender. Make sure it
fits tightly. Turn blender on low speed first, then up to high and
puree until smooth. Turn off the blender. Add lemon juice and sugar.
Put the lid on again and blend.
4. With a rubber spatula, spread the fruit puree as thinly as possible
onto a non-stick baking sheet.
5. Bake in the oven for about 25 minutes.
6. Using a potholder, transfer the baking sheet to a cooling rack.
Allow to cool, then peel the fruit off of the sheet and eat!
Makes 1-2 servings.

Darth Maul Dip

This recipe can easily be doubled or tripled for a party.

INGREDIENTS

1	jar (15 ounces) roasted red peppers
1	small clove garlic, peeled
1	teaspoon red wine vinegar
$1/2$	teaspoon salt
$1/2$	teaspoon pepper
1	tablespoon cream cheese
$1/4$	cup poppy seeds
	Corn chips or crackers

1. With a colander or sifter, drain the peppers. Lay them flat on a piece of paper towel. Blot the peppers to dry them as much as possible. Remove any pieces of blackened skin.

2. Place the peppers and all remaining ingredients except the poppy seeds in a blender or food processor and blend until smooth.

3. Use a spatula to spread the dip evenly onto a flat plate. Chill the dip for 1 hour.

4. Remove the chilled dip from the refrigerator and sprinkle the poppy seeds over it evenly.

5. Place the dip on the table and drape a black cloth around the plate to make Darth Maul's cape.

6. Serve with corn chips or crackers.

Makes 1 $1/2$ cups

Main Courses

Galaxy Grilled Cheese

Padmé Pad Thai

Nabooli Forest

Opee Sea Crunch

Sando Aqua Monster Soup

Darth Double Dogs

Pit Droid Pizza

Protocol Droid Pasta

Greedo's Burritos

Han-Burgers

Obi-Wan Kebabs

Crazy Cantina Chili

TIE Fighter Ties

Boba Fett-uccine

Galaxy Grilled Cheese

INGREDIENTS

4   slices whole-wheat bread

4   teaspoons butter, at room temperature

8   thin slices Cheddar cheese

8   pickle slices

1. Lay 1 slice of bread on a work surface. Spread one side with 1 teaspoon of the butter. Repeat with the remaining bread slices and butter.
2. Turn 2 bread slices over so the buttered sides are down. Top the slices with the cheese slices, dividing them evenly.
3. Lay 4 pickle slices on top of each stack of cheese. Top with the other 2 bread slices, buttered sides up.
4. Place the sandwiches in a skillet. Set the skillet on the stove and switch on the heat to medium. Cook the sandwiches until golden brown on the underside and the cheese begins to melt, about 3 minutes. To check, lift up a corner of a sandwich with a spatula and peek underneath. Using the spatula, flip over both sandwiches. Cook until golden brown on the second side and the cheese has melted, about 3 minutes longer.
5. Use the spatula to transfer the sandwiches to a cutting board. You can cut your sandwiches into stars or planets if you have a star-shaped or round cookie cutter. Press the cookie cutter straight down into the sandwich. Be careful not to burn your fingers on the hot cheese. Lift the cutter gently. Repeat with the other sandwich. Serve the sandwiches immediately.
Makes 2 sandwiches.

Padmé Pad Thai

Here is a quick and easy dish disguised as a gourmet meal. You won't believe how easy it is to whip up a plateful of these flavorful noodles... and neither will your trusted decoy.

INGREDIENTS

¼   pound dried rice noodles (banh pho)

4   tablespoons vegetable oil

2   cloves garlic, chopped

¼   cup water

2   tablespoons fish sauce

1   tablespoon brown sugar

1   teaspoon paprika

¼   teaspoon cayenne pepper (optional)

10 to 15 shrimp, cooked, peeled and deveined

4 to 6   scallions cut in inch-long pieces

4   tablespoons roasted peanuts, coarsely chopped

2   cups bean sprouts

1   lime cut into wedges

1. Soak the noodles for two hours in cold water or ½ hour in hot water. Drain.

2. Measure and chop all the ingredients and set them near the stove.

3. Heat the oil in a wok or large nonstick skillet over medium heat.

4. Add the garlic and stir for a minute.

5. Add the noodles. Cook them for about three minutes, stirring constantly and pulling them apart.

6. Add the water, fish sauce, sugar, paprika, and cayenne pepper, stirring to coat all the noodles.

7. Add the shrimp, scallions, peanuts, and bean sprouts.

8. Keep stirring and cook for about three more minutes.

9. Serve with lime wedges on the side for squeezing over the top.

Serves 2 to 4

Nabooli Forest

Here's the Naboo version of a tabouli-style salad. Fill the celery "trees" with your favorite spread and perch them in the landscape. And make that forest thick — you'll need all the protection you can get when the Trade Federation starts their invasion.

FOREST FLOOR

1	teaspoon olive oil
1/4	cup diced yellow onion
1/2	teaspoon garlic powder
1/2	teaspoon salt
1	teaspoon lemon juice
1 1/4	cups water
1	cup instant couscous
2	tablespoons chopped fresh parsley
1	tablespoon chopped fresh mint

CELERY TREES

8	celery stalks with leaves
1/2	cup hummus, cream cheese, or peanut butter

1. In a saucepan, heat the olive oil over medium heat. Add the onions and sauté for 5 minutes.
2. Add the garlic powder, salt, lemon juice, and water, and bring to a boil.
3. When liquid is boiling, add the couscous. Cover and remove from heat.
4. Allow to stand for 10 minutes, remove cover, add the parsley and mint, and fluff with a fork.
5. Meanwhile, cut four of the celery stalks to the same length. Cut the other four stalks to the same length also, but longer than the first four.
6. Fill four of the stalks with your favorite filling.
7. Match each stalk with its mate and squeeze together.
8. Stand the celery trees up in mounds of Nabooli and enjoy!

Opee Sea Crunch

This delectable fish filet has a galactic crunch you won't be able to resist. Just watch out behind you — there's always a bigger fish!

INGREDIENTS

1	cup corn flakes
1/2	cup crispy rice cereal
2	tablespoons flour
1	teaspoon salt
1	egg
2	teaspoons water
1	pound fresh or frozen boneless catfish, sole, or bass filets
	Tartar sauce

1. Preheat oven to 350°F.

2. In a bowl, mix the cereals together and crush with your fingers into a coarse meal.

3. In a second bowl, mix the flour and salt together with a fork.

4. In a third bowl, whisk the egg and water together until smooth.

5. Take a fish filet and dredge it through the flour, coating evenly. Then place the floured fish in the egg wash and quickly coat both sides. Next, lay the coated fish filet in the cereal mixture. Carefully lay the fish on a baking sheet lined with parchment or foil. Repeat with the remaining fish filets.

6. Bake for 20 minutes. Fish should be cooked through and the breading lightly browned.

7. Remove from oven and serve with tartar sauce.

Serves 4

Sando Aqua Monster Soup

Deep in the recesses of your soup bowl, hiding behind chunks of celery and carrot, lies the sando aqua monster. Slurp with caution!

INGREDIENTS

1	large can (49 ounces) chicken stock
1	large jicama, peeled
1	cup chopped celery
2	large carrots, peeled and sliced into rounds
	salt and pepper to taste
1	teaspoon fresh thyme leaves (or $1/2$ teaspoon dried)
1	large can (10 ounces) chicken meat, drained (or 1 cup cooked chicken meat, chopped)

1. In a large stockpot, bring the chicken stock to a boil.
2. Cut the peeled jicama in half. Set one half aside and dice the other into $1/2$ inch squares. You should have about 1 cup diced jicama.
3. When the stock is boiling, place the chopped vegetables in the pot and boil for 10 minutes.
4. Remove from heat and add the salt, pepper, thyme, and chicken.
5. Cover the pot.
6. Have an adult carve the sando aqua monster out of the other half of the peeled jicama. Lay the jicama on the flat side. Cut four legs out of the bottom, then trim the rest of the jicama away to leave a long, slender body with four legs and a long tail (see photo).
7. Place the sando aqua monster into a large glass bowl. Carefully ladle the hot soup into the bowl and place it in the middle of the dining table.
8. Serve the soup with a ladle, but be careful not to be caught by the sando aqua monster!
Serves 4

Darth Double Dogs

Once you get a grip on these, you'll never go back to the single dog again.

INGREDIENTS

8   foot-long hot dogs

1   package refrigerator crescent dinner rolls

4   long wooden skewers

1. Preheat oven to 375°F.

2. Take a wooden skewer and skewer it halfway into one of the hot dogs, then take another hot dog and skewer it onto the other end. You will have one long hot dog held together with a skewer. Repeat with the remaining hot dogs.

3. Open the dinner roll package and unroll. The rolls will be perforated into triangular shapes. Detach them two at a time so you have four rectangles of dough.

4. Place one double hot dog on the edge of the rectangle, centering it. Roll the dough around the hot dog. When you get to the other side of the rectangle, gently press the hot dog down to seal the dough edge. Repeat with the three other double hot dogs.

5. Place hot dogs on a baking sheet and bake for 12 to 15 minutes, or until dough is golden brown. Remove from oven and allow to cool.

6. Serve with ketchup and mustard. Be careful when eating these — they are like a corn dog with a stick in the center.

Makes 4 double dogs

Pit Droid Pizza

Rumor has it that Watto's pit droids build these pizzas when they're not working on his Podracer. If they're in a hurry, they use prepared pizza sauce.

PIZZA SAUCE

1	tablespoon olive oil
¼	cup chopped onions
½	teaspoon minced garlic
4	tomatoes, diced
2	tablespoons tomato paste
¼	cup water
½	teaspoon each dried basil, oregano, and thyme, or double the amount of fresh, chopped
1	teaspoon salt
½	teaspoon pepper

PIZZA

1	cup fresh pizza sauce
1	pre-baked pizza crust
½	cup mushrooms, sliced
¼	cup black olives, sliced
20	pepperoni slices
1	cup shredded mozzarella

1. Preheat oven to 375°F.
2. In a large saucepan, heat the olive oil over medium heat until hot. Add the onions and garlic and sauté for 6 minutes, or until the onions are soft. Add the tomatoes, tomato paste, and water, bring to a boil, then reduce heat to a simmer.
3. Cover the sauce and simmer for about 15 minutes, until thick.
4. Add the herbs, salt, and pepper, and stir. Remove from heat.
5. To assemble the pizza, spread 1 cup sauce on the center of the crust, leaving ½-inch or so around the edges.
6. Sprinkle half the mushrooms, olives, and pepperoni evenly on top of the sauce.
7. Sprinkle the mozzarella over the pizza.
8. Arrange the remaining toppings on top of the cheese. You may sprinkle additional herbs on top as well.
9. Bake on a pizza pan or cookie sheet for 15 to 20 minutes, or until cheese is melted and sauce is bubbly.
One pizza serves 3-4

Protocol Droid Pasta

Oh, my! C-3PO's parts are definitely showing in this delightful dish. Have fun decorating your pasta à la C-3PO, and don't forget the photoreceptors. A protocol droid needs to see!

INGREDIENTS

4	ounces dried multi-colored pasta (cappelini or spaghetti is best)	1	teaspoon salt
1	can (14 $\frac{1}{2}$ ounces) low-fat chicken stock	2	slices white or sourdough bread
2	cauliflower florets (fresh or frozen)		Olive oil
1	cup water		Garlic salt
	Pinch of turmeric	1	tablespoon parmesan
		2	pine nuts

1. Prepare the pasta according to package instructions.
2. While the pasta is cooking, pour the chicken stock into a sauté pan and bring to a simmer. Cook for 4 to 6 minutes, until the stock is reduced by half.
3. Place the cauliflower, water, and turmeric in a pan and boil for 5 minutes on the stove.
4. Turn on the oven broiler or toaster oven. With a knife or kitchen shears, trim one slice of bread into the shape of C-3PO's head plate and the other into a mouth plate. Brush both sides of each piece with olive oil, sprinkle with garlic salt, and toast in oven until browned.
5. When the pasta is cooked, drain and place it in a large bowl. Pour the reduced chicken stock over the pasta and sprinkle parmesan and salt on top. Using tongs, toss the pasta until coated. Mound the pasta onto a plate in a face shape.
6. When the cauliflower is cooked, place the florets slightly above the center of the face for eyes. Place a pine nut in the center of each floret to make pupils.
7. Place the garlic toast head and mouth plates as shown.
8. Sprinkle with additional parmesan and enjoy!
Serves 2

Greedo's Burritos

INGREDIENTS

1	can (14-ounces) black beans
1	cup grated Monterey Jack cheese
1/2	head iceberg lettuce
1	tomato
1	tablespoon olive oil or vegetable oil
1 1/2	pounds lean ground beef
4	flour tortillas, each about 10 inches in diameter
1/2	cup sliced black olives

1. Get an adult to help you with this recipe!

2. Preheat oven to 350°F.

3. Open the can of beans and drain the liquid into the sink. Set aside.

4. Put the iceberg lettuce on the cutting board cut side down. Cut the lettuce from top to bottom in narrow slices. Now cut across the slices, again in narrow strips. Set aside.

5. Put the tomato on the cutting board. Cut out the green stem. Then cut the tomato in half from the top to the bottom. Holding a tomato half cut side down, slice it crosswise about 1/2-inch thick. Now cut the slices into little cubes. Set aside.

6. Put the oil in a skillet. Put the skillet on the stove and switch on the heat to medium high. When the oil is hot, carefully add the beef. Cook, stirring often, until browned, about 15 minutes.

7. Wrap the tortillas in aluminum foil and place in the oven to heat, about 5 to 10 minutes.

8. Meanwhile, add the beans to the beef and continue to cook, stirring often, until the beans are heated through, about 2 minutes. Turn off the heat.

9. Using pot holders, remove tortillas from the oven. Place a tortilla on a plate. Spoon one-fourth of the beef mixture onto the tortilla. Sprinkle with one-fourth of the cheese. Top with one-fourth each of the olives, the tomato, and the lettuce. Roll up the tortilla around the filling.

10. Repeat step 9 until all the ingredients are used up.

Makes 4 burritos.

Han-Burgers

Han Solo is generally right-handed, but is known to fire a ketchup blaster with his left hand. (Condiments always taste better when blasted onto one's food.)

INGREDIENTS

1	pound ground lean beef
1	teaspoon salt
$1/2$	teaspoon pepper
1	teaspoon Worcestershire sauce
4	tomato slices
4	whole-wheat hamburger buns
	Lettuce leaves, pickle slices, ketchup, and mustard for serving

1. Put the ground beef, salt, pepper and Worcestershire sauce in a bowl. Using your hands, mix them together until well blended.
2. Divide the meat mixture in 8 equal portions. Form the portions into 8 patties $1/4$-inch-thick.
3. Place 1 tomato slice on 1 patty. Top with another patty. Use your fingers to press the edges together to seal. Repeat this step to make 4 filled patties.
4. Put a large skillet on the stove and switch on the heat to medium. When the skillet is hot, after about 1 minute or so, carefully put the hamburgers in the pan. Cook until browned on the underside, about 6 minutes. To check, lift a corner of the burger with the spatula and peak underneath. Flip over the hamburger and cook on the second side until browned and cooked through, about 6 minutes longer.
5. Use the spatula to transfer the burger onto the bun. Serve with lettuce leaves, pickle slices, ketchup, and mustard—blasted on, of course!
Makes 4 Han-burgers.

Obi-Wan Kebabs

INGREDIENTS

2	chicken breasts
4	small red new potatoes
3	zucchinis
3	ears of corn
	Olive oil

1. Get an adult to help you with this recipe!

2. Soak 8 wooden skewers in water for 30 minutes.

3. Preheat the oven to 375°F.

4. Put a chicken breast on a cutting board. Using a knife, cut the meat in 1-inch strips. Now cut across the strips to make 1-inch cubes. Repeat with remaining chicken breast. Set chicken aside.

5. Wash the cutting board and knife thoroughly with soap and warm water. Rinse and dry the cutting board.

6. Put a small potato on the cutting board and cut it in half. Repeat with remaining potatoes and set aside.

7. Put a zucchini on the cutting board. Trim off the stem and the base. Then cut the zucchini into 1-inch rounds. Repeat with the remaining zucchini and set aside.

8. Put an ear of corn on the cutting board. Cut the corn into 1-inch rounds. Repeat with remaining corn.

9. Very carefully push one round of corn onto the skewer. Follow with a potato half, chicken cube, and zucchini slice. Begin again with the corn and continue until there are only 2 inches left on the skewer.

10. Using a pastry brush, brush the meat and vegetables with olive oil and sprinkle with salt and pepper.

11. Grill or broil until vegetables are tender and chicken is cooked through, turning frequently, about 30 minutes.

Makes 8 kebabs.

Crazy Cantina Chili

INGREDIENTS

1	can (16-ounces) kidney beans
1	can (16-ounces) black beans
1	can (16-ounces) garbanzo beans
1	onion
2	tablespoons vegetable oil
2	tablespoons chili powder
1/8	teaspoon cayenne pepper
1	can (28-ounces) crushed tomatoes with juice
1	cup tomato juice
	Salt and pepper to taste
	Shredded Cheddar cheese
	Sour cream or plain yogurt

1. Open the cans of beans. Drain off the liquid from the cans into the sink. Set the beans aside.

2. Put the onion on a cutting board. Carefully slice off the root end and the stem end. Use your fingers to strip off the dry skin. Then cut the onion in half from the top to the bottom. Hold an onion half cut side down and thinly slice it crosswise. Now hold the slices together and cut across them in the opposite direction. Be sure to keep your fingers clear of the knife blade. Set aside.

3. Put the oil in a large saucepan. Set the pan on the stove and switch on the heat to medium-high. When the oil is hot, add the chopped onion and stir with the wooden spoon until tender, about 5 minutes.

4. Add the chili powder and cayenne pepper and stir for 30 seconds.

5. Add the beans, the crushed tomatoes, and the tomato juice. Stir well. Reduce heat to medium low and simmer for 15 minutes, stirring occasionally. Season to taste with salt and pepper.

6. Serve the chili with the cheese and sour cream on the side.

Makes 4 to 6 servings.

TIE Fighter Ties

These galactical finger-foods are sure to start a battle in your very own kitchen: a battle over who takes command of the fresh-from-the-oven fleet of TIE Fighter Ties!

INGREDIENTS

4	pre-cooked sausages or hotdogs, approximately 5-inches long
1	package refrigerator breadsticks (8 breadsticks)
	Ketchup and mustard

1. Preheat the oven to 350°F.
2. Cut sausages in half crosswise. Set aside.
3. Open the package of breadsticks and separate the lengths of dough.
4. Cut the lengths in half and set aside. You should have 16 lengths of dough when you are finished.
5. Place one sausage half, cut-side down, on a baking sheet.
6. Take 1 length of dough and wrap it around the base of the sausage half. Cross the ends and let them fall on the baking sheet in the form of the letter V. Using another length of dough, wrap the same sausage in the opposite direction. Cross the ends and let them fall in the form of an upside-down V. Repeat with remaining dough and sausage halves.
7. Bake according to breadstick package directions, or until dough puffs up and turns golden brown.
8. Using pot holders, remove from the oven. Serve with ketchup and mustard.
Makes 8 TIE Fighter Ties.

Boba Fett-uccine

INGREDIENTS

1	small head broccoli	$1\frac{1}{2}$	cups bottled pasta sauce
1	small head cauliflower	3	quarts water
1	small zucchini	$\frac{1}{2}$	pound fettuccine noodles
3	teaspoons salt		Grated Parmesan cheese

1. Put the broccoli on a cutting board. Using a knife, cut off the florets (the flowery-looking tops). Measure one cup of florets. Repeat this step with the cauliflower.

3. Put the zucchini on the cutting board. Trim off the stem and the base. Then cut the zucchini into thin rounds.

4. Fill a medium saucepan three-fourths full with water. Add $1\frac{1}{2}$ teaspoons of the salt. Put the pan on the stove and switch on the heat to high. When the water boils, slowly add broccoli, cauliflower, and zucchini. Cook until tender, about 4 minutes.

5. Turn off the heat. Place colander in the sink. Remove the pan from the stove and pour the water and vegetables into the colander. Be very careful; steam can burn you.

6. Return the vegetables to the saucepan. Pour in the pasta sauce. Set the pan on the stove and switch on the heat to medium. Heat, stirring occasionally with a wooden spoon, until hot. Turn down the heat to very low.

7. Now pour the 3 quarts water into a large saucepan. Add the remaining $1\frac{1}{2}$ teaspoons salt. Put the pan on the stove and switch on the heat to high. When the water boils, slowly add the fettuccine and stir once or twice with a wooden spoon. Boil until tender, about 8 minutes or according to package directions.

8. Turn off the heat. Remove the pan from the stove and carefully pour the water and pasta into the colander.

9. Transfer the noodles to a large serving bowl. Pour the sauce over the top. Sprinkle with Parmesan cheese and serve.

Makes 2 to 3 servings.

Desserts and Treats

Wookiee Cookies

INGREDIENTS

2 1/4 cups all-purpose flour	
1	teaspoon baking soda
1	teaspoon salt
1	teaspoon ground cinnamon
1	cup unsalted butter, at room temperature
1	cup packed brown sugar
1/2	cup granulated sugar
2	large eggs
1 1/2 teaspoons vanilla extract	
1	cup milk chocolate chips
1	cup semi-sweet chocolate chips

1. Preheat the oven to 375°F.
2. Put the flour, baking soda, salt, and cinnamon in a mixing bowl. Stir with the wooden spoon until well mixed. Set aside.
3. Put the butter, brown sugar, and granulated sugar in another mixing bowl. Using the electric mixer set on high speed, beat together until well blended and creamy, about 3 minutes. (You can do this with a wooden spoon, but it will take longer.) Beat in the eggs and vanilla extract. Add the flour mixture and stir with the wooden spoon until blended. Stir in the chocolate chips.
4. Scoop up a rounded tablespoonful of the dough and drop onto a baking sheet. Repeat until you have used up all the dough. Be sure to leave about 1 inch between the cookies because they spread as they bake.
5. Using pot holders, put the baking sheets in the oven. Bake until golden brown, about 10 minutes.
6. Again, using pot holders, remove the baking sheets from the oven. Lift the cookies from the baking sheets with a spatula, and place on cooling racks. Let cool completely.
Makes about 3 dozen cookies.

Bossk Brownies

Bossk the bounty hunter never caught his quarry, Han Solo and Chewbacca. Perhaps he was distracted by these delicious brownies.

INGREDIENTS

	Butter for greasing baking dish
$2/3$	cup all-purpose flour
$1/2$	cup unsweetened cocoa powder
$1/2$	teaspoon baking powder
$1/2$	teaspoon salt
$1/2$	cup unsalted butter, at room temperature
$1/2$	cup packed brown sugar
$1/2$	cup granulated sugar
2	large eggs
1	teaspoon vanilla extract
$1/2$	cup white chocolate or butterscotch chips

1. Preheat the oven to 350°F. Butter an 8-inch square baking dish.
2. Put the flour, cocoa powder, baking powder, and salt in a small bowl. Stir with a wooden spoon until well mixed. Set aside.
3. Put the butter, brown sugar, and granulated sugar in one large bowl. Using the electric mixer set on high speed, beat together until well blended and creamy, about 3 minutes. (You can do this with the wooden spoon, but it will take longer.) Beat in the eggs and vanilla extract. Add the flour mixture and stir with the wooden spoon until blended. Stir in the white chocolate or butterscotch chips.
4. Pour into the prepared baking dish and smooth the top with a rubber spatula.
5. Using pot holders, put the baking dish in the preheated oven. Bake until a toothpick inserted into the center comes out clean, about 25 minutes.
6. Again using pot holders, transfer the dish to the cooling rack. Let cool completely.
Makes about 16 brownies.

Death Star Popcorn Balls

Like the Empire's deadly Death Star, making popcorn balls can be very dangerous. Do not dare to make them without the help of an adult.

INGREDIENTS

1/3	cup popcorn kernels	1	teaspoon vinegar
3	cups sugar	1	teaspoon vanilla extract
1 1/2	cups water		Butter or vegetable
1/2	cup light corn syrup		shortening for
1/2	tablespoon salt		greasing hands

1. Get an adult to help you with this recipe!

2. Pop the corn using whatever method you prefer.

3. Put the sugar, water, corn syrup, and salt in the saucepan. Stir well with a wooden spoon. Clip a candy thermometer on the side of the pan. Set the pan on the stove and switch on the heat to low. Add the vinegar and vanilla and cook, stirring constantly, until the thermometer reads 270°F.

4. Get an adult to carefully pour the hot sugar mixture over the popcorn and toss with two large spoons to coat every kernel. Allow to cool slightly.

5. Rub butter or vegetable shortening on your hands so the popcorn won't stick to them. Then scoop up enough popcorn to form a ball about the size of a baseball.

6. Shape the ball with your hands.

Makes 2 to 3 popcorn balls.

Wampa Snow Cones

Luke was imprisoned by a ferocious wampa on the ice planet Hoth, and held captive in the creature's frozen lair. Narrowly escaping with his life, some believe Luke also made off with the wampa's secret snow cone recipe.

INGREDIENTS

2	cups fresh or thawed frozen blueberries
¼	cup water
1	tablespoon sugar

1. Put the blueberries in a bowl. Mash them with a fork until there's lots of liquid.
2. Hold a strainer over a small glass baking dish and pour the mashed berries into a sieve. Press the berries with a fork to push through as much liquid as possible.
3. Add the water and sugar to the blueberry juice. With a wooden spoon, stir until the sugar dissolves. Put the dish in the freezer.
4. After 30 minutes take the dish out of the freezer. Stir the mixture with a fork to break up the crystals. Return the dish to the freezer for another 30 minutes.
5. Remove the dish again and break up the crystals one more time. Return to the freezer and freeze until firm, about 4 hours.
6. Remove the dish from the freezer. Using the fork, scrape the mixture into small crystals. Quickly scoop the crystals into small paper cups and serve right away.
Makes 2 servings.

Variation: Replace the blueberries, water, and sugar with a bottled fruit juice or drink such as apple juice, lemonade or punch. Follow the directions for freezing and scraping the crystals.

R2-D2 Treats

R2-D2 never eats, or so it seems. These frozen treats were discovered in a freezer at the abandoned Rebel base on Hoth. Did they belong to R2-D2? We can only guess...

INGREDIENTS

1/2	cup white chocolate chips
2	tablespoons chopped peanuts
1	banana
1	Kit Kat® candy bar

1. Line a baking sheet with waxed paper.
2. Put the chocolate chips in a small, heavy saucepan. Put the pan on the stove and switch on the heat to low. Stir constantly until the chocolate is melted and smooth. Remove from heat and set aside.
3. Peel the banana. Put on a cutting board and cut into 4 equal pieces.
4. Place the peanuts in a small bowl. Break the Kit Kat® into four bars. Cut each bar in half and set aside.
5. Dip 1 banana piece in the melted chocolate. Dip just the top of the banana piece into the peanuts.
6. Place the banana piece nut side up on the lined baking sheet. Press 2 Kit Kat® pieces along either side of the banana.
7. Repeat steps 5 and 6 with the remaining banana pieces.
8. Place the baking sheet in the freezer until chocolate has hardened, about 15 minutes. Serve straight from the freezer.
Makes 1 or 2 treats.

Sandtrooper Sandies

INGREDIENTS

3/4	cup butter, at room temperature
1 1/4	cups sugar
2	eggs
1	teaspoon vanilla extract
2	cups all-purpose flour
1/4	teaspoon salt
	Vegetable oil for greasing the baking sheet
	Confectioners' sugar

1. Put the butter in a bowl. With an electric mixer set on high speed, beat the butter until soft and light in color.

2. Gradually add the sugar in a slow, steady stream, and beat until creamy and lemon yellow. Then add the eggs one at a time, beating well after each addition. Add the vanilla and stir just until blended.

3. Put the flour and salt into a sifter and sift them into a small bowl. Slowly add the flour mixture to the butter mixture, beating it in with the electric mixer on low speed until it is fully incorporated. The dough will become very stiff and you may have to knead the last bit of flour in by hand. With your hands, pat the dough into a ball and flatten the ball into a thick disk. Wrap the dough in plastic wrap and chill in the refrigerator for 1 hour.

4. Preheat an oven to 400°F. Lightly oil a baking sheet.

5. Remove dough from the refrigerator and unwrap. Dust your work surface with flour. With a rolling pin, roll out the dough 1/4-inch thick.

6. Using cookie cutters of any shape you like, cut cookies out of the dough. Carefully transfer the cookies to the oiled baking sheet, leaving a little space around each one. Gather up any dough scraps, roll them out again, and cut out more cookies.

7. Slip baking sheet into the oven and bake until cookies just begin to brown, 8 to 10 minutes. Using pot holders, carefully remove the baking sheet from the oven. Transfer the cookies to cooling racks with a spatula and allow them to cool. Sift a little confectioners' sugar over the cookies.

Makes about 3 dozen cookies.

Watto-melon Cubes

Jedi mind tricks won't work on that tough-talking Toydarian, but these luscious cubes of melon just might. Take a chance on these juicy treats and let fate decide.

INGREDIENTS

$1/2$ large seedless watermelon

Blue decorating sugar

1. Cut the watermelon into 2-inch-wide round slices. Trim away the rind. Cut the melon into 2-inch-square cubes.
2. Gently dab each side of the cubes on a paper towel to dry them slightly.
3. Pour the blue decoration sugar onto a plate.
4. Dip two sides of each cube into the sugar and place on a small plate, four cubes per serving.

Serves about 4

Anakin's Apple Crisp

The prophecy refers to the one who will bring balance to the Force, and there's nothing like yummy home-cooked food to give a kid a chance. You'll find that Shmi's original recipe produces a delectable dessert.

TOPPING		FILLING	
20	pecan shortbread cookies	4	large green apples
1/2	cup flour	3	tablespoons flour
1/2	teaspoon nutmeg	1/4	cup sugar
1 1/2	teaspoons cinnamon	1	teaspoon cinnamon
1/2	cup cold butter, cut into small pieces		

1. To make the topping, place the cookies in a zip-lock bag and crush them with a rolling pin into coarse crumbs.
2. Place the crushed cookies, flour, spices, and butter in a large bowl. With a fork or your fingers, crumble the ingredients together until the mixture has the consistency of pea-size clumps. Set aside.
3. Preheat oven to 375°F. Butter an 8 1/2 x 11-inch glass baking dish.
4. Peel and core the apples. Cut them into 1/4-inch slices, then cut the slices into wedges.
5. In a large bowl, toss the chopped apples, flour, sugar, and cinnamon together. Place the mixture in a baking dish.
6. Top the mixture with the crumble topping, making sure to completely cover the apples.
7. Bake for 30 to 35 minutes, until the topping begins to brown and the apples are bubbling.
8. Serve warm with vanilla ice cream or whipped cream.
Serves 6 to 8

Qui-Gon Jinn-ger Snaps

According to Qui-Gon himself, these cookies are an energizing nibble — the perfect pick-me-up for those times when you aren't busy battling destroyer droids or outrunning assault ships.

INGREDIENTS

4	cups flour		2	sticks butter
1	tablespoon ginger		$2/3$	cup brown sugar
1	teaspoon cinnamon		2	large eggs
1	teaspoon nutmeg		$2/3$	cup molasses
1	teaspoon salt		$1/4$	cup apricot jam
$1/2$	teaspoon baking soda		2	tablespoons powdered sugar

1. In a large bowl, mix the flour, sugar, spices, salt, and baking soda together.

2. In a separate bowl, beat the butter and sugar with a mixer until light and fluffy. Add the eggs and beat until creamy. Add half the dry mixture to the butter mixture and beat until well blended. Pour in the molasses and beat until mixed. Scrape down the sides of the mixer bowl, add the remaining dry mixture, and mix until well combined.

3. Wrap the dough in plastic wrap and chill for at least 1 hour.

4. Preheat oven to 350°F. Line two cookie sheets with parchment paper.

5. On a floured surface, roll out the dough $1/4$ inch thick with a rolling pin.

6. Cut the cookies into rounds with cookie cutters. To make the door that Qui-Gon cuts through with his lightsaber, use the largest round cutters, and with a knife, cut small crescent shapes out of the center of half the cookies.

7. Bake for 12 to 15 minutes for softer cookies, 20 minutes for crispy ones. Remove from oven to cool.

8. While the cookies are baking, whisk the apricot jam and powdered sugar together until smooth.

9. After the cookies have cooled, spread $1/2$ to 1 teaspoon of the filling on half of the cookies, placing another cookie on top to make a sandwich. Place the cookie with the crescent on top.

Makes approximately 20 small cookie sandwiches

Panakacakes

It's a good thing the palace tower wasn't actually made of these delicious, peanut-buttery cakes. Amidala and Panaka may not have been able to resist a nibble, and would have been delayed in their efforts to capture the viceroy.

INGREDIENTS

2 cups flour	1/2 cup milk
1/4 cup brown sugar	1 egg
2 1/2 teaspoons baking powder	Whipped cream or vanilla ice cream
1/4 teaspoon salt	Your favorite chocolate sauce
1 stick cold butter, cut into small pieces	
1/4 cup creamy peanut butter	

1. Preheat oven to 400°F. Line a baking sheet with parchment paper.
2. In a large bowl, sift the dry ingredients together.
3. With a fork or your fingers, crumble the butter and dry ingredients together until a coarse meal forms. (Pieces of butter are okay.)
4. In a small bowl, whisk the peanut butter, milk, and egg together until smooth. Pour into the dry ingredients and mix with a fork just until dry ingredients are moistened. Do not overmix.
5. Pour the dough onto a floured work surface and press dough into a rectangle, 3/4 inch thick. With a knife, cut the rectangle into eight small rectangles. Transfer the small rectangles to the baking sheet with a spatula.
6. Bake for 20 minutes, or until light brown.
7. Serve with whipped cream or vanilla ice cream and chocolate sauce. You can also stack the shortcakes one on top of the other, layering the chocolate sauce and whipped cream between them. Then, with a serrated knife, cut slices from the Panakacake "wall" and serve.

Serves 6

Hideous Sidious Sorbet

Here's the scoop: icy and cold as the Sith Lord himself, this sorbet is surprisingly sweet. But like Sidious, it has the power to melt away without a trace.

INGREDIENTS

½	cup sugar
3	cups frozen blackberries, drained
½	cup berry Italian soda syrup (any kind of berry will work)
2	tablespoons lemon juice
½	cup heavy cream
1	sheet grape or berry fruit leather

1. In a blender, purée the sugar and berries until smooth. Strain the purée to remove seeds. Rinse the blender, and pour the berry purée, syrup, lemon juice, and heavy cream into it. Blend until mixed.
2. Freeze in an ice-cream maker according to manufacturer's instructions.
3. To serve, place two scoops of the sorbet in a bowl. Cut the fruit leather into four equal pieces. Drape the fruit leather over the sorbet, 1 piece per bowl, to resemble Darth Sidious's hood.
Serves 4

Darth Vader Dark Chocolate Sundaes

Some speculate that Darth Vader was lured to the Dark Side by these Dark Chocolate Sundaes.

INGREDIENTS

$1/2$ cup bottled hot fudge sauce

1   quart chocolate ice cream

$1/2$ cup whipped cream

4   tablespoons chopped nuts

4   teaspoons chocolate chips or chocolate sprinkles

1. Put the hot fudge sauce in a small, heavy saucepan. Put the pan on the stove and switch on the heat to low. Stir constantly until the sauce is melted and smooth. Remove from the heat.
2. Set out 4 bowls. Put 2 scoops of ice cream into each bowl.
3. Top each serving with about 2 tablespoons hot fudge. Top with the whipped cream and sprinkle each serving with 1 tablespoon nuts and 1 teaspoon chocolate chips or sprinkles.
Makes 4 servings.

Variations: You can use any flavor ice cream or sauce that you like. Other toppings besides peanuts might include M&Ms, mini marshmallows, fresh berries, or shredded coconut.

Drinks

Sith Slush

Skywalker Smoothies

Jawa Jive Milkshakes

Yoda Soda

Bibble Bubble

Sebulba's Sinister Cider

Mini-chlorian Concoction

Darth Malt

Hoth Chocolate

Sith Slush

This tart red spritzer with blueberry ice cubes echoes the sinister colors of Darth Maul himself. Picture Sidious and Maul cooling off after a long, hot day on the dark side with tall, frosty glasses of sparkling Sith Slush — cheers!

INGREDIENTS

½	cup blueberries or blackberries
1	can lemon-lime soda
¼	cup cranberry juice or fruit punch

1. In a blender, blend the berries until smooth. If not completely blended, add ¼ cup water. Pour the blended fruit into ice-cube trays and freeze.

2. When the fruit cubes are ready, mix the soda and juice together in two large glasses. Place two or three frozen fruit cubes into each glass and serve.

Serves 2

Skywalker Smoothies

Luke definitely has the Force on his side, but sometimes he gets an extra boost from these scrumptious smoothies.

INGREDIENTS

1	cup fresh or frozen strawberries
1	banana
1/2	cup pineapple, grape, or orange juice
4	Ice cubes

1. If you are using fresh strawberries, cut off their stems with a knife. Put the fresh or frozen berries in a blender.
2. Peel the banana. Break it into pieces and add them to the blender. Then add the fruit juice and ice cubes.
3. Put the lid on the blender. Make sure it fits tightly. Turn on the blender first at low speed, then increase to high speed. Blend until smooth and frothy, 1 to 2 minutes. Turn off the blender and wait until it stops. With a wooden spoon, check to see that the fruit is thoroughly blended. If not, repeat this step.
4. Pour into 2 glasses and serve immediately.
Makes 2 servings.

Variation: Add a scoop of vanilla or berry frozen yogurt to the blender along with the other ingredients.

Jawa Jive Milkshakes

Jawas are famous for scavenging abandoned ships, droids, and scrap metal. When they get together at giant swap meets, they allegedly serve these delicious shakes.

CHOCOLATE-BANANA

2   cups vanilla ice cream or frozen yogurt

1   banana, peeled and broken into pieces

$1/2$ cup milk

$1/4$ cup chocolate syrup

$1/2$ cup crushed Heath® Bars (optional)

VANILLA AND PEANUT BUTTER

1   cups vanilla ice cream or frozen yogurt

1   teaspoon vanilla extract

$1/2$ cup milk

$1/4$ cup creamy peanut butter

$1/2$ cup peanut butter chips

SUPER STRAWBERRY

2   cups strawberry ice cream or frozen yogurt

1   cup frozen strawberries

$1/2$ cup milk

$1/2$ cup white chocolate chips (optional)

DOUBLE CHOCOLATE

2   cups chocolate ice cream or frozen yogurt

$1/2$ cup milk

$1/4$ cup chocolate syrup

$1/2$ cup crushed chocolate sandwich cookies (optional)

1. Select the milkshake you want to make. Assemble the ingredients for your recipe. (Tip: The best way to crush the cookies or candy bar is to put them in a clean, sturdy plastic bag and roll a rolling pin back and forth over them.)

2. Put all the ingredients into a blender.

3. Put the lid on the blender. Make sure it fits tightly. Turn on the blender first at low speed, then increase to high speed. Blend until smooth, 1 to 2 minutes.

4. Pour the milkshake into 2 glasses. Serve each shake with a spoon and a straw.

Makes 2 milkshakes.

Yoda Soda

Jedi Master Yoda levitates Luke's X-wing from the Dagobah swamp in *The Empire Strikes Back*. Here he peacefully levitates a frothy glass of Yoda Soda.

INGREDIENTS

3   limes

3   tablespoons sugar, or more to taste

1   cup sparkling water

1   scoop lime sherbet or sorbet

1. Place 1 lime on the cutting board and cut it in half. Squeeze the juice from each half into a measuring cup. Repeat with the remaining limes until you have ¼ cup juice.
2. Put the lime juice and 3 tablespoons sugar in a small pitcher. Stir with a wooden spoon until the sugar dissolves. Add the sparkling water and stir until mixed. Taste and add more sugar, if desired.
3. Using an ice cream scoop, scoop up the sherbet and drop it into a tall glass. Pour in the lime water. Serve immediately.
Makes 1 serving.

Variation: You can substitute rainbow sherbet or lemon sorbet for the lime sherbet.

Bibble Bubble

Poor Sio Bibble had a tough job holding his own against Nute Gunray and Daultay Dofine. Rumor has it he calmed the nervous Niemoidians with a constant supply of this effervescent concoction.

INGREDIENTS

2	sugar cubes
1	tablespoon grape juice or Italian soda syrup
2	cans plain soda water

1. Place the sugar cubes on a soup spoon.
2. Carefully pour the grape juice or syrup all over the sugar cubes until they are soaked but still hold their cube shape.
3. Pour the soda water into two glasses.
4. Drop a soaked sugar cube into each glass.
5. After the sugar dissolves, drink with a straw.

Serves 2

Sebulba's Sinister Cider

A cup of this steamy spiced cider will keep you hot under the collar, just like the dangerous Dug. It's a cozy warm-up on a cold winter's night.

INGREDIENTS

4	cups apple juice
1/2	teaspoon nutmeg
5	cinnamon sticks
4	whole cloves
	Whipped cream

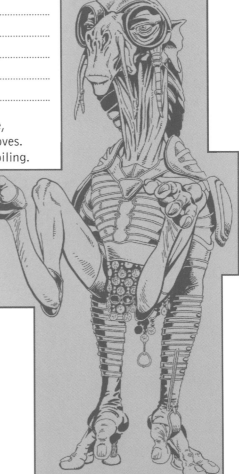

1. In a large saucepan, combine the apple juice, nutmeg, one of the cinnamon sticks, and the cloves. Gently heat the cider for 10 minutes without boiling.
2. Place one cinnamon stick in a mug. Ladle cider into the mug, leaving the cloves in the saucepan. Repeat with three more mugs, and top each with whipped cream.
3. After the cider has cooled a bit, drink through the cinnamon-stick "straw."
Makes 4 servings

Midi-chlorian Concoction

For a midi-chlorian count that's off the charts, we recommend a healthy helping of this tasty shake.

INGREDIENTS

1	banana
1/4	cup creamy peanut butter
1	teaspoon cocoa powder
2	teaspoons sugar
1 1/2 cups milk	

1. Slice the banana into a blender.
2. Add the remaining ingredients and blend 1 minute, or until smooth.
3. Serve in two chilled glasses.
Serves 2

Darth Malt

This milkshake is sinfully good, and the subtle malty flavor holds a certain mystery. Just a few velvety sips will prove how simple it would be to take the quick and easy path to the dark side.

INGREDIENTS

6	malted milk balls
2	large scoops vanilla ice cream (or your favorite flavor)
¾	cup milk

1. Place the malted milk balls in a heavy plastic bag. With a rolling pin or mallet, crush the milk balls into small pieces.
2. Pour all ingredients into a blender and mix on low speed until smooth and creamy.
3. Pour into your favorite glass and enjoy.
Serves 1

Hoth Chocolate

The Rebellion's hidden Echo Base on the ice planet Hoth was freezing! Sometimes the Rebels wished they could just warm up with a mug of this Hoth chocolatey drink.

INGREDIENTS

1	cup milk
2	heaping teaspoons sugar
1	heaping teaspoon unsweetened cocoa powder
1/8	teaspoon vanilla extract
	Small marshmallows (optional)

1. Pour the milk into a small saucepan. Add the sugar, cocoa powder, and vanilla to the milk. Stir vigorously with a whisk until the sugar and cocoa dissolve.
2. Place the pan on the stove and switch on the heat to medium. Watch for tiny bubbles to appear along the edge of the pan, then immediately remove the pan from the heat.
3. Carefully pour into the mug and serve immediately with marshmallows, if desired.
Makes 1 serving.

Index

Index